MY CANADA

NEW BRUNSWICK

Weigl

Published by Weigl Educational Publishers Limited
6325 10th Street SE
Calgary, Alberta T2H 2Z9

Website: www.weigl.ca

Library and Archives Canada Cataloguing in Publication

Goldsworthy, Kaite, author
     New Brunswick / Kaite Goldsworthy.

(My Canada)
ISBN 978-1-77071-868-5 (bound).
ISBN 978-1-77071-869-2 (pbk.)

     1. New Brunswick--Juvenile literature. I. Title. II. Series: My Canada (Calgary, Alta.)

FC2461.2.G65 2013   j971.5'1   C2013-902394-1

Printed in the United States of America in North Mankato, Minnesota
1 2 3 4 5 6 7 8 9 0 17 16 15 14 13

052013
WEP040413

Project Coordinator: Megan Cuthbert
Art Director: Terry Paulhus

Weigl acknowledges Getty Images as the primary image supplier for this title.

We acknowledge the financial support of the Government of Canada through the Canada Book Fund for our publishing activities.

2

Contents

This is New Brunswick.
It was named for King
George III of Great Britain.
He was also called the
Duke of Brunswick.

This is the shape of New Brunswick. New Brunswick is bordered by the United States and the Atlantic Ocean.

New Brunswick sits between Quebec and Nova Scotia.

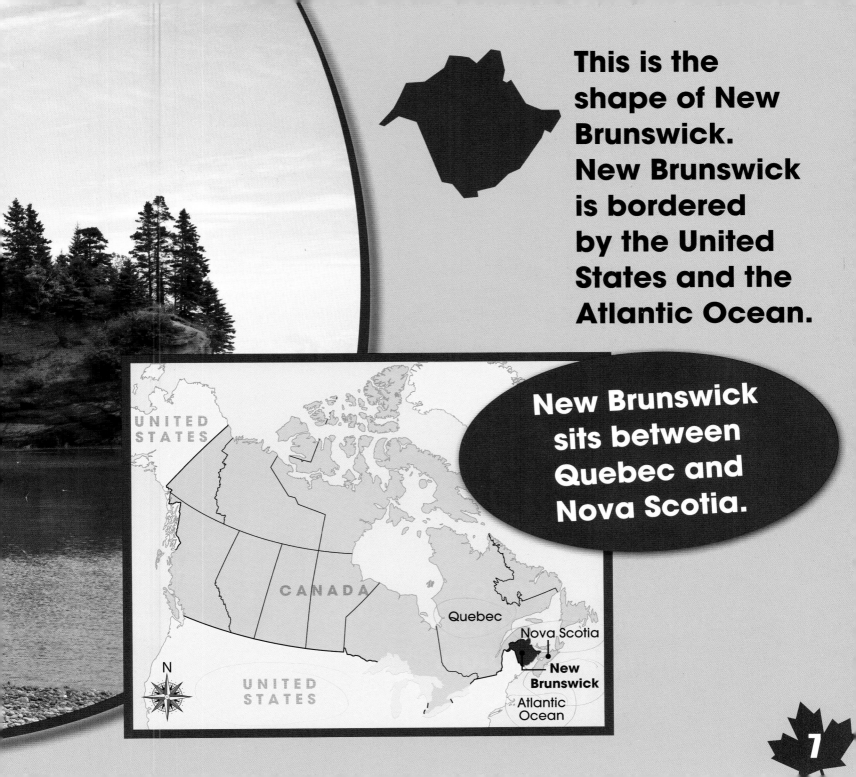

UNITED STATES

CANADA

Quebec

Nova Scotia

New Brunswick

Atlantic Ocean

UNITED STATES

N

Fredericton is the capital city of New Brunswick. In the past, many British soldiers lived and worked there.

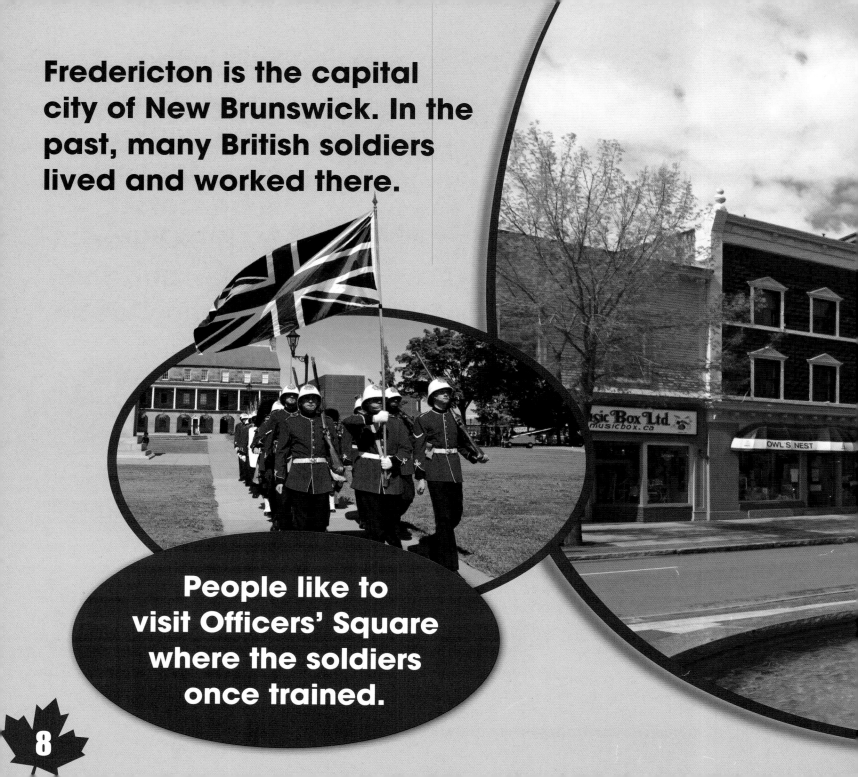

People like to visit Officers' Square where the soldiers once trained.

9

People came from France and England to live in New Brunswick. The two countries fought many times for the province.

Many people in New Brunswick speak both French and English.

The province's coat of arms has a yellow shield with a ship on it. A salmon and two white-tailed deer surround the shield. The deer are standing on violets and fiddleheads.

SPEM REDUXIT

Fiddleheads are a type of vegetable that grows in New Brunswick.

This is the flag of New Brunswick. It is yellow with a ship sailing on it. Across the top is a gold lion on a red background.

Many ships were built in New Brunswick. The ship on the flag is called a galley.

The flower of New Brunswick is the purple violet. It grows in wet meadows and woodlands.

The black-capped chickadee is New Brunswick's official bird. Chickadees are named for the sound they make.

17

New Brunswick has many salmon farms. People from around the world buy salmon from New Brunswick.

Restigouche Sam, the world's largest salmon, is in Campbellton.

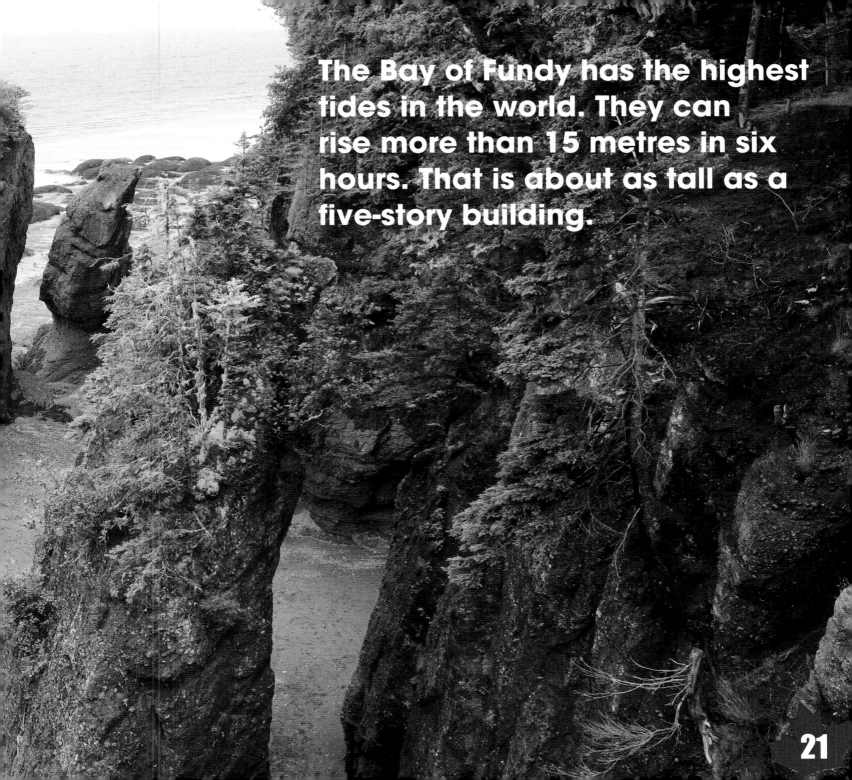

The Bay of Fundy has the highest tides in the world. They can rise more than 15 metres in six hours. That is about as tall as a five-story building.

NEW BRUNSWICK FACTS

These pages provide detailed information that expands on the interesting facts found in the book. They are intended to be used by adults as a learning support to help young readers round out their knowledge of each province and territory in the *My Canada* series.

Pages 4–5

New Brunswick is the largest Maritime province, with an area of 72,908 square kilometres. It has a population of about 756,000. It was one of the original four provinces of Canada after Confederation. Moncton is the largest city in the province. New Brunswick's main industries include mining, fishing, agriculture, forestry, and tourism.

Pages 6–7

The Gaspé Peninsula of Quebec is north of New Brunswick, the Bay of Fundy is to the south, and the Gulf of St. Lawrence is to the east. The province is joined to Nova Scotia by a piece of land called the Chignecto Isthmus. The 12.9 km-long Confederation Bridge joins New Brunswick to Prince Edward Island. It is one of the longest bridges in the world.

Pages 8–9

Fredericton has a population of about 94,000. The Saint John River runs through the middle of the city. Fredericton became the provincial capital in 1785. It is named after Prince Frederick, son of King George III. The Historic Garrison District in Fredericton was home to British soldiers from 1784 to 1869. It was declared a National Historic Site in 1964.

Pages 10–11

New Brunswick was settled by France in the early 1600s. The Maritime region was named Acadia. Battles with Great Britain for control of the area resulted in France finally losing the region to the British in 1755. As a result, 5,000 Acadians were forced to leave the area. New Brunswick is the only officially bilingual province in Canada.

Pages 12–13

On New Brunswick's coat of arms, the provincial shield is supported by white-tailed deer wearing collars with flags that represent Great Britain and France. An Atlantic salmon wears St. Edward's Crown. It sits on a coronet of gold maple leaves. The motto at the bottom means "hope restored."

Pages 14–15

The flag was adopted in 1965. Its design is based on the province's shield of arms. The coat of arms was given by Queen Victoria in 1868. The galley represents the province's history of shipping and shipbuilding. The lion represents the province's link to Great Britain.

Pages 16–17

The black-capped chickadee is approximately 12 to 15 centimetres long. It has at least 15 different calls, but the best known is the one for which it it named. The purple violet grows in wet areas, reaching a height of 12 to 25 centimetres. It was adopted as the official provincial floral emblem in 1936.

Pages 18–19

After British Columbia, New Brunswick is the largest salmon producer in the country, accounting for almost 40 percent of Canada's salmon. Atlantic salmon is the largest food export from the province. Restigouche Sam is an 8.5 metre metal sculpture located along the Restigouche River in Campbellton.

Pages 20–21

The Bay of Fundy is a 270-km-long bay that stretches between New Brunswick and Nova Scotia. During one tide cycle, 100 billion tonnes of seawater move in and out. There are usually two low and high tides each day. Within six hours, the vertical tides in the bay cause the areas to go from sand to water that is 15 metres deep.

KEY WORDS

Research has shown that as much as 65 percent of all written material published in English is made up of 300 words. These 300 words cannot be taught using pictures or learned by sounding them out. They must be recognized by sight. This book contains 47 common sight words to help young readers improve their reading fluency and comprehension. This book also teaches young readers several important content words, such as proper nouns. These words are paired with pictures to aid in learning and improve understanding.

Page	Sight Words First Appearance
4	also, for, he, is, it, named, of, the, this, was
7	and, between, by
8	city, in, like, many, once, people, there, to, where
11	both, came, from, live, times, two
12	a, are, has, on, with
13	grows, that
15	were
17	make, sound, they
19	around, farms, world
21	about, as, can, more, than

Page	Content Words First Appearance
4	Duke of Brunswick, Great Britain, King George III, New Brunswick
7	Atlantic Ocean, Nova Scotia, Quebec, shape, United States
8	Fredericton, Officers' Square, soldiers
11	countries, England, English, France, French, province
12	coat of arms, fiddleheads, salmon, shield, ship, violets, white-tailed deer
13	vegetable
15	background, flag, galley, lion, top
16	flower, meadows, woodlands
17	bird, black-capped chickadee
19	Campbelltown, Restigouche Sam
21	Bay of Fundy, building, hours, metres, tides